DO YOU HEAR ME, GOD?

Len Coverston

DO YOU HEAR ME, GOD?

Ruth and Arthayer Sanborn

THE JUDSON PRESS, VALLEY FORGE

DO YOU HEAR ME, GOD?

In memory of
DAVID
whose untimely death
made us kin to
suffering humanity

Words are nothing but

    lives lived,
    complaints shared,
    heartaches mended,
    loved ones buried,
       ill ones comforted,
       tiredness eased,
       tensions loosened,
          a wanderer guided.

Thank you

    for sharing
    such lives
    with us.
          The SANBORNS

CONTENTS

Prayer is the people talking with **God.**

It takes place as the sun
    shreds the morning horizon
        or under the radiance
            of a noonday sun
        or even
            in the mists of twilight.

Prayer is MAN talking with GOD!

Prayer is listening, too.

It is God addressing us
    through all the events in our lives,
        no matter how important
            or insignificant they may be.

It is the Lord meeting us on every step of our lives—
    at home,
    at school,
    at work,
    at play;
        in our automobiles,
        in our offices,
        in our factories,
        in our churches;
            when someone is born,
            when someone falls in love,
            when someone marries,
            when someone dies.

Prayer is the people talking with God.
Prayer is the people listening to God.
Prayer is the people doing God's work
    here on earth!

I'M AFRAID, LORD!

Jesus came to make men whole. But it takes time to heal. It also takes faith. His spirit can make us whole when we are ready to let him work in us.

Slow me down, Lord, slow me down.
   I guess
      I've wanted too much,
      too soon,
         and here I am
            on the junk heap of life!

Slow me down, Lord, slow me down.
   I guess
      I had to try everything once.
       Look at me, Lord,
          on the junk heap of life!

Slow me down, Lord, slow me down.
   Somehow
      I learned to hate, Lord,
         and distrust,
         and fear.
            So I started to run, Lord,
            and now
            I can't stop.

Slow me down, Lord, slow me down.
   They tell me
      You died for ALL of us, Lord.
         Is that true?
      In this battered body of mine, Lord,
         is there something
         worth saving?
      In this tortured mind of mine, Lord,
         are there thoughts
         worth thinking?
      In this breaking heart of mine, Lord,
         can healing
         take place?

Slow me down, Lord, slow me down.

It is hard enough to know the will of God but harder still to accept it. But when we do accept it, God breaks through with the peace that passes understanding.

God —
    I asked: "How long have I got to live?"
        and the doctor said:
            "About a year."

                      An alley cat strolled
                      along a wall
                      beside a fence —
                      an open fence.
                      And I could see
                      a man with hammer,
                      nails and screws,
                      trying to fix
                      a backyard door.

Look, God, they neither of these know of me or care!

                      My life, my pain,
                      my health, my death;
                      they do not know,
                      nor feel, nor care.

Yes, God, I know —
    I have no life save
        as you deign to give me life.

I knew all this before,
but
never did it have meaning.
Now it's real.
A YEAR TO LIVE!

"Thy will be done."
'Tis all I know to say.
But, if it be
a year,
or two,
or ten,
or twenty —

Thank you, God,
that I have been
exalted — lifted up —
a moment
in your time
and your eternity!

Prayer may not put us in a different place to remove our burdens, but it can deliver us from ourselves and the pain of indifference so that God can act through us whenever we learn to love others as we love ourselves.

God —

the pain never leaves me.

I'm depressed,
my head throbs,
my heart pounds,
I cannot face myself,
for today
I saw
poverty,
ragged children,
deprived old age,
eyes without hope,
loneliness,
hunger,
and then
I rode back
into affluence.

God —

the pain never leaves me.

I want to keep what I have.
And then I want more.
My pantry is full.
I can't seem to share.

What more
is there
to say?

God —

the pain never leaves me.

19

God intends to disturb us and make us discontented. How can we live in our world and be content? How can we live with ourselves and be content? God expects something more of us—action that changes things!

I'm not sure, God, that I like what's happening to me.

> Last night
> as I lay on my cot
> I realized
> how much I hate,
> how alone I am,
> what a fool I've been,
> how I long for
> something good
> to happen to me
> so I'll change.

I'm not sure, God, that I like what's happening!

> Yes, I went to the chapel.
> For the first time
> I looked at myself
> and I disliked what I saw;
> I looked for a friend
> and I was alone;
> I tried to be honest
> and admit I'd been a fool.
> But it's not easy, God;
> it's just not easy!

I'm not sure, God, that I like what's happening.

    Yes, I heard the chaplain.
      He told us
        about your love.
          How could you die,
          Lord, for the
          likes of me?
          Are you a fool,
          Lord, to think
          it could make
          a difference?

I'm not sure, God, that I like what's happening.

The mercy of the Lord is not just for us, but for all.
He is the Lord of all humanity. He knows no boundary
of nation, race, or people. He crosses enemy lines to
share himself with all. And we must share him, too.

    Lord, I am only one mother,
      but tonight
        I multiply myself by many thousands.

My boy
is far away
on the other side
of the world;
lonely,
overburdened,
tired,
perhaps
facing
death.
He is all the soldiers in the world.

I am only one mother, Lord,
but tonight
I multiply myself by many thousands.

He is
seeing
suffering,
heartache,
degradation,
turmoil,
death.
He is all the oppressed in the world.

I am only one mother, Lord,
but tonight
I multiply myself by many thousands.

There's a glow
on the horizon!

Is it YOU, Lord?

We don't like pain and we suffer from it. Then why are we so careless about inflicting pain on others and on God? In suffering there is much to be learned and much to be shared.

The Lord is my shepherd, I shall not want . . .

> They're all the words I know, Lord,
> and they do help some.

He leadeth me beside the still waters . . .

> It's a burning pain, Lord.
> The waters
> would cool
> my body, Lord.
> I'm so tired . . .

He restoreth my soul . . .

> It's a little easier now, Lord.
> Thank you, Lord.
> I promise
> I won't ask you
> "why" anymore.
> I won't ask
> why this illness
> came to me.
>
> I've tried to do right.
> I've tried to help people.
> I've tried to go to church.
> I've tried to be a friend.
> I've tried . . . YES, I HAVE!

Oh, Lord, please take it away.
TAKE AWAY THE PAIN!

Yea . . . yea though I walk
through the valley
of the shadow
of death . . .

Lord — take away the pain!

Take away the . . .

Thank you, nurse.

GOD, I'M TRYING TO LISTEN

In the place where we are—what does the gospel mean?
How are we fulfilling his command to GO and DO?

God,

I have been listening to your gospel.

It is comfortable to sit in your house.
It is easy to listen to your gospel.
It is pleasing to sing your praises.
It is so helpful to hear the words.

BUT

It is difficult to live what YOU ask:

"Feed the hungry, and
    love your brother.
Clothe the naked, and
    love your brother.
Visit the sick, and
    love your brother."

HOW CAN I DO THESE THINGS?

God,

I am well fed,
    well clothed,
        well housed,
            well educated.

God —

IS YOUR COMMAND FOR EVERYONE?

God does not desert; he desires. He does not hide from us, but seeks us. Can it be that we look for him in the wrong places? We flee from him because we fear his judgment. Can it be that we do not hear because we're making so much noise?

God —

    Why can't I pray?

    Why is it so hard to find the words
        to say to you?
            Words that will bring me
                into your sight?
            Words that will open
                the secrets of my heart?

God —

    Why can't I pray?

God —

    Why can't I find you?
    Why are you so far from me when I need you
        to quiet my soul?
            So far from me when I am helplessly
                orbiting in my own sorrow?
            So far from me in the muddy trench
                of self pity?

God —

Why can't I find you?

WHAT'S THAT, GOD?

> *Lo, I am with you always*
> *even unto the end of*
> *the world!*

God —

Was that YOUR voice?

Words are but symbols by which we express our
thoughts. But prayer is more than words—it is the shar-
ing of our most intimate everyday experiences with a
God who listens and responds. What and how do we
communicate with him?

God —

What is prayer?

> Is it bowing my head?
> Is it getting on my knees?
> Is it looking inward?

No, my child, it is
none of these.

But, God —

I feel so desolate!
I NEED to pray.

Is it bowing my head?
Getting on my knees?
Looking inward FOR thee?

God —

Is that YOUR voice I hear?

My child,
it is not just
these things.
It must be more!
LISTEN!

You must not fear silence.
Dialogue with me
requires silence.

You must not stand still.
Standing still
is disobedience!

31

Care for the sick,
Stay with the dying,
Visit the prisoner,
Clothe the naked,
Feed the hungry.

Then you will be
talking with me, for
Prayer to be total must be
combined with action.

What does God see in our minds? What is he trying to show us? Are we groping or growing? Are we content or concerned? Are we blinded by comforts or can we see the needs which surround us?

Lord, make me aware
of walls which block my view
and stunt my faith;
of thoughts which shrink my mind
and limit my vision.

Lord, make me aware
of racial crises,
of youthful delinquency,
of hungry people,
and cold,
and loneliness,
and being afraid.

Lord, make me aware
of all I have;
of friends and family,
of church and community,
of freedom and a full stomach,
and of little things like
clothes,
and furnaces,
and hot water,
and supermarkets.

Lord, make me aware
of YOUR gospel's message:

"Do unto others . . ."
"Who is my neighbor . . ."
"And who will go for us . . ."
"And the greatest of these is love . . .

Lord, make me aware!

In an issue of Guideposts, *Arthur Godfrey tells about a blacksmith who once prayed: "Put me in the fire, Lord, if that's what it takes. Just don't throw me on the scrap heap." Can we relate these words to ourselves today!*

God —

Some days it's hard to understand
why life brings problems
and suffering.
I know some people wonder
why so much comes to them,
and why their friends seem
to get by
with
little or
no trouble.
I asked myself about this last night, God,
and
I suddenly realized
I don't really know much about
other people's burdens.
I only know about my own!

Thank you, God, for my burdens.

Now that I'm growing older,
I can see that
they have helped me mature.

I once saw through the glass darkly,
    but now
        I seem to know that
           this is the way
           your refining fire works.

So, Lord, "put me in the fire
    if that's what it takes.
        Just don't throw me on the scrap heap!"

        I still have a lot I want to do.

We do not have to measure the bounty of God; we only have to use it. We may not understand how he works, but we must accept what he does!

God —
    The sky is windswept,
        The air frosty and biting;
           yet the sun rises earlier and
           casts its warmth a little longer
               across the tired shoulders of the earth.

I have to tell you, God,
    about the quietness
        in the early morning.

There's a hushed silence,
sometimes made restless
by the beating
of a winter's storm.

As YOU listen, God,
can you, too, hear the stirrings?
It may be a rivulet of water
as the sun melts an icicle
along the eaves of time.

Or the softness of the bird's call
against the deep azure
of a cold, blue sky.

Or the silkiness of a sudden breeze
let loose as the cold wind
sleeps for a moment.

God — I have to tell you: "Thank you!"

The promise is there.
Life does not die to go unheeded.
It stirs again deep in the
bowels of the earth
until the noise of life
o'ertakes the cold, the wind.

Thank you, God,
for helping me crack relentless winter
with the warmth of your promise.

HOW COULD YOU LOVE ME SO MUCH?

The world isn't what it used to be. Something has hap-
pened to men, and we don't know what it is. We're
squeezed together in the struggle for survival and in the
search for life's meaning—and—what has happened to
God?

God —

    it seems that I have failed.

      I am man.
      And man,

         selfish,
         proud,
         destructive,
         arrogant,

           has sent YOUR SON
           again
           to the Cross.

I sit in church.
      I pray.
         I think I listen.

           And then,
           out I go
           to live as
           I want,
           not
           as YOU say.

God —

it seems that I have failed.

The world hates me.
The world says that you are dead.

And if you are,

I have killed you
with my indifference.

GOD!

It often takes the troublesome burden, the unresolved problem, the despair of the soul, before we search out God's understanding. But he is there. He has revealed his power and his presence; he has offered his will and his wisdom. Maybe we have ignored his offer and have been trying to meet the demands of life alone. Let us stop and listen to what he has to say to us, because HE DOES CARE.

God —

sometimes

you take a soul
and
make it listen for a moment . . .

sometimes

> you take a moment
> and
> make it change a life . . .

sometimes

> you take a life
> and
> make it an influence for good.

God —

sometimes

> I wonder
> why
> you care
> so much.

Youth cries out:
          I WANT TO BE ME, LORD!

God makes men restless. It is only then that they will go out in search of the real meaning of life with all of its complications and its demands.

Hey, You —

What can I do?

I'm so bored.
What am I supposed to do?

School is a prison, and
I don't want to learn, but
this is all I hear:

gotta go to college . . .
study for college boards . . .
don't you want to succeed? . . .

43

What can I do?

I'm so bored.

No place to go!
Look at me!

I don't know who I am;
I don't know where I'm going.
I don't even know
where I've been . . .
and I don't care!

I just want something to do!

School is out.

WHAT CAN I DO?

Can't go home.
No one there.
Can't stand on the corner.
"Scram, you kids, no loitering!"

Don't want to study.
Don't have a girl.
Don't even know who I am!

Hey, You —

I JUST DON'T KNOW!

What can I do?

Life is to be shared. It is a combination of age and youth, wisdom and wishing, prayer and problems, counsel and conflicts, love and labor, endurance and growth. How do we share them?

God —

    It's so hard to understand why
        my parents
            yell at me;
            argue with me;
            don't trust me;
            are afraid for me;
            don't understand me.

            Some of it must be my fault.
            But it's hard to see it!

    Help me to realize
        my parents'
            great "givingness,"
                and their need for my love, too;
            their intense concern,
                yet their need for my caring;
            their restrictions,
                yet their desire for my freedom;
            their humbleness when I remember
                to show them those little courtesies;
            their pleasure when I don't forget
                to be willing.

Thank you, God,
>for parents who
>>let me invite my friends,
>>let me borrow their car,
>>give me a good home, and
>>>all the food I can eat.

>>They DO love me,
>>they DO care.

>>I guess
>>it isn't easy
>>to bring up me!

The meaninglessness of life is painful. It happens when a man is afraid to look at life as it really is. The Christian cannot try to escape reality—he must wrestle with it.

God —

I don't know why I'm talking to you.
I don't really believe you're out there.
I don't believe anything I can't see.
>And I sure can't see you, so
I don't know why I'm talking to you.

God —

There's only one thing
I really want to do.

I want to pull down a shade and
shut out the world.

Why?

Well,

I guess it's because
nothing's going right.

I'm afraid,
I'm a failure,
I'm mixed up,
I'm lonely.

No one understands me,
no one cares,
no one wants me,
no one sees my problems.

God —

I don't know why I'm talking to you.

I only want to pull down a shade and
shut out the world.

Do YOU really hear me?

God — really?

Do you hear me?

Sin separates man from God, and man is lost. But God does not give up. He keeps reaching out in love, offering forgiveness, and is ready always to welcome us back. He keeps calling us to repentance. Why don't we accept his offer?

Big Man upstairs —
    I'm lost
    I'm lonely
    I'm broken!

        You seem to hear
        all the other people
        who talk to you!
            What's the matter with me?
            Ain't I good enough for you?
            Don't you approve of me?

            You gave me my wearied Pa,
            you gave me my tired old lady,
                and it looks as though
                    you stuck me in this
                    lousy town.

Big Man upstairs —
    I'm sick of being hunted.
        I'm tired of being blamed
        for all that goes wrong around me.
            I'd like a job
            and some decent clothes,
            and a warm house,
                and to know where's
                my next meal!

Big Man upstairs —
Isn't there anything left for me?
Must I always keep running?
Isn't there enough to go around?
Must I always be hungry?
Isn't there any peace?
Must I always be a sewer rat?

Big Man upstairs —

Wonder who that is
standing
in the next block?

What?

YOU put him there?

Perhaps our prayers are empty because we ask God to make our choices for us, and he doesn't. He has already chosen us and provided for us. But we must choose how we will use what he has given.

Lord,
I've been thinking
about the choices
which I have to make.

Friends,
heroes,
clothes,
college,
movies,
TV programs.

These are little things
but
there are big things, too.

I've heard all the words of wisdom —
I've been given all the counsel —
Now I have to choose.

And it's hard, Lord,
believe me,
it's hard.

How can I know
Your will in my life?
How can I keep from drifting
into the wrong thing?

Should it be

teaching,
writing,
nursing,
law,
business,
medicine,
secretary?   What? ? ? ? ?

Should it be

San Antonio?
St. Louis?
New York?
Boston?
Africa?
Vietnam?
Montgomery?   Where? ? ? ? ?

Lord,

I've been thinking
about the choices
which I have to make.

Something that will
bring meaning, Lord!

Something that will
use me, Lord, to
Thy glory!

My child,

It may take you
into the garden;

it may take you
to your knees;

it may take you
to Calvary!

. . . and parents plead:
WE NEED YOUR HELP, LORD!

*Too many of us forget the things we should remember,
and remember the things we should forget. But what we
remember and forget determines our life together.*

Heavenly Father,

    Help me to understand

        the compulsiveness,
        the frustration,
        the selfishness,
        the intense desires

        that fill my child's whole being.

Remind me
of when I, too, was young!

How I hated,
and loved,
and played,
and procrastinated,
and followed my friends,
and played my cards so that
I could have my own way!

Give me

patience to understand,
unselfish love,
wisdom to guide,
a knowledge that
my teaching, over these few years,
may be remembered
when he needs it most!

Thank you, God,
for my child's life.

May my little
be the beginning
of a strong
foundation.

Life does not allow us to lean on yesterday's comforts
or to drift in tomorrow's currents. Each generation must
live in its own time. As we look at the pieces of our
lives, let us pray for humble spirits that will dare to
talk with God and then listen to his offer of help. But
what good is his help unless we are willing to accept it?

Oh God,

> we give them so little, really,
>> these children of ours.

We tell them:

> wait — I'm busy . . .
> be quiet, I'm talking . . .
> pick it up . . .
> lay it down . . .
> study . . .
>> practice . . .
>>> go and do . . .

but

> *we* don't wait,
> *we* aren't quiet,
> *we* don't pick up,
> *we* don't go
>> and
>>> do.

Oh God,

> we give them so little, really,
>> these children of ours.

And yet

they grow in YOUR image until

the world claims
them. And then
we wonder
how
we failed them.

Oh God,

help them to do better than we have done.

Most of those who give up do not lack strength and ability, but vision and motivation. Prayer does not often give the answers to the problem—it empowers one to find the answers!

Heavenly Father,

Help me to climb over this problem.

Strengthen me
so I will not look back,
for I know
what fear is.

Place my eyes on the course,
     not on the height
     of the climb.

Give me courage to look
at one step only.

          It is so much easier —
          one step at a time.

          It is so much easier
          when YOU are there
          helping to carry
          the load.

Heavenly Father,

     Help me to climb over this problem.

God is love. And he has shown us how to love. As we love ourselves, we must love others, for this is HIS command. But this is hard, isn't it?

     Oh, God —

          What's happened to our marriage?
          What's happened to
               the love that glowed within us
               for each other?

the faith we had
in one another?
the dreams we had built
for a long future together?
the home we had started?
the trust
we had in each other's goodness?

God — WHAT HAS HAPPENED TO IT?

There's a wall between us!

We no longer discuss;
we only disagree.
We no longer share;
we are only selfish.
We no longer live for the other;
we think only of ourselves.

And all of this —
this not caring,
nor sharing,
nor loving,
we show to our children.

God — what has happened?
Where have we failed?

God — lead us back to YOU!
God — take us, please!

God does care what happens to us. That is why he came to live among us so he could heal the broken-hearted, bind up men's wounds, and set men free. But we have to let him perform his miracle of healing in us!

My God,

This is too heavy a burden.

When the call came
I couldn't believe.
I wouldn't believe,
but the voice kept insisting,
so here I stand.

The sky is barren;
the whispering pine is moaning;
the bird on the wing is leaving me;
the brown earth shudders beneath me;

and

I must throw my life
on your mercy.

for you have handed me this burden,
yet you sent me the gift.

You thought me strong enough
to give life,
yet
it seems as though
you have taken it away.

Was I unworthy?
Was I a failure?
Didn't I love enough?
Didn't I try hard enough
to shape the clay
in YOUR image?

God —

This is too heavy a burden.

WHY DID MY CHILD HAVE TO DIE?

*The hidden things are important. For instance, the
power that produces the roots of a tree, the current of
a river, the thoughts of a man. Think of what happens
when the power fails!*

God —
I thought about you today
as I washed a window.
I got out the ladder
and the cloths and cleaner,
and scrubbed and scrubbed.

It took a long time
for it to come clean,
and it wasn't until

I got out more cloths,
and more cleaner
and washed the inside, too,
that I could see through the pane.

God —
my life's like that, too —
dirty on the inside
as well as on the outside.

I try to keep what people see
clean and neat, but
some days
I'm shriveled inside,
and miserable, too.

I guess the window of my soul
needs scrubbing!

God —
I can't just live a life of contemplation.
There's too much work to be done, but

let me look at my tasks through
the eyes of the spirit;
let me commune with you so that
my windows come clean;
then I can see through the problems
to their solving.

God —
Is that snow I see on the mountaintop?

The Christian faith does not let us ignore the facts of life. It makes us face them. It doesn't give any easy answers or glib promises. Rather, it sends us out to climb every mountain with the determination that God's way does work. But we must apply his truth to every situation. And this makes it difficult!

Lord,

    the words came to me over the radio:

        "Just across tomorrow's mountain . . ."

            The rest of the song
            disappeared in the mists,
            for I stood
            before that mountain.

My wife is ill;
    my son smashed the car;
        my daughter has a new boyfriend
        and
        I don't like him, Lord!

            I don't know why —
            these are just
            little things, Lord,
            but
            they are my mountain!

Lord,

    I've tried all the cliches:

Don't worry, tomorrow's another day . . .
Every cloud has a silver lining . . .
The sun never sets but it rises again . . .
Your luck will turn . . .

                    but
                    none of them work.

Lord, what about YOU?

        Across my mountain, Lord,

                    are you there?
                    Do you care?

                        Sshhhhhhh!
                        Listen!

But
    It's a young man's world and
        all around it
            he seeks,
                he reaches,
                    he even fights
                        and sometimes
                            he dies.
            IS IT WORTH IT, LORD?

From the beginning of time, men have been curious about their fellowman, but they have also feared him. Instead of seeing him as a brother, they have too often thought of him as an intruding stranger. Instead of welcoming his differences, they have been suspicious of him. But God has made only ONE nation and ONE human family. Jesus' deepest prayer was that "they might all be one." If we want freedom in our world, we must be ready to treat all men as brothers.

Lord —

It's been more than a month since I left home.
Already there are moments when I look forward to the day
    when, once again,
        I shall step on my native soil.

This country has a raw beauty.
There are lofty peaks,
broad plains,
dense jungles,
intense heat,
and the wettest rain
I have ever known.

My country has beauty, too.
My country has freedom!

This country has NOTHING.

I'm proud, Lord, that I can be here
helping this country
find its place
in the freedom circle.

For there must be
room for all!

This I have learned,
in one short month.

Lord —

Not just food on MY TABLE,
but food on my brother's!
Not just a bed for me,
but a bed for my brother!
Not just work for me,
but worthwhileness for my brother!

Our shadow reaches farther than we know. It falls on the pathway of those we pass by. Our spirit and our deeds, too, leave an imprint on other lives. The little things we thought unimportant may one day become meaningful to another. Someone may be following our example. They may be learning about life from us. Their faith may be destroyed or strengthened as they see our faith demonstrated. It's a great responsibility, isn't it?

God —

I've been thinking about
all the things which I remember:

My home,
my town,
and especially
my church!

Sunday morning in the Church school;
our teachers challenging us to think!
The congregation singing
"Faith of Our Fathers."
Shaking hands before service.
The fun in youth fellowship.
The smell of Easter lilies
and Christmas candles.

They're memories.
They bless and burn.

God —

I'm trying to make memories here, too,
so that I can share with those at home
the beauty of this country,
the poverty and heartache,
the problems and the hopes,
the culture of a strange people.

I'm growing, too, and I suddenly know why.
It's because my roots are deep
in family love,
in understanding teachers,
in a church that cares —
and the roots are nurtured
by their prayers.

Thank you, God, for my church —
for my home —
for my school.
Thank you, too, for the freedom
which is my country.
Thank you that she is not afraid
to stand up for that
which she believes.
Thank you for my country's
opportunities.

A person really learns
over here
what it means
to be a Christian.

I cannot make this journey alone, God.
I am counting on you to show me the way.

72

Sometimes our doubts have a way of making us search for the truth. Sometimes things we have neglected become terribly important. Sometimes the only way God can teach us is by placing us in a position where we have to learn. Sometimes God must become impatient with us because it takes us so long to learn. . . .

Lord —

I'm sitting just ten feet away from a dead soldier.
 He's not more than twenty-one.
 He'll never draw another breath.
 He'll never think again of home.

I think of his family.
 How will they feel when the word comes?
I think of my country.
 Why doesn't it appreciate its freedom?
I think of the poverty in this country.
 Why do we HAVE and they DON'T HAVE?

  Have you, in our heritage, Lord,
   made the difference?
  If YOU have, Lord, why is there
   so much
    hatred
     in people's hearts?

I think of the pain, Lord,
    of the wounded and dying.
I think of the pain of desolation
    in the hearts of these people.
I think of the pain in my own heart
    as it is often gripped with fear.
I think of the pain of love which is so great
    that it brings loneliness to my parents.

Lord —

    this boy won't go home again.
        But I want to go home when this is over.
        I have so much I want to do.

Lord —

    I think about all of these things.

        Help me to keep going!

Those who make the most out of life are those who dare to make their way into the unknown. The explorer, the pioneer, the reformer—each in his turn had to abandon the frustrations of the past and brave the dangers of the unknown. Only then could they uncover the things that were waiting to be discovered. Could it be that we never get to the richest things in life because we are afraid to go and find what God has already put in our world?

Lord — I'm afraid.

My emotions are overwhelmed by fears.
I guess fear is common in
a soldier's life.

We are not only fighting an enemy, Lord,
We are fighting our own emotions.
We are meeting our hopes and anxieties
on a new plane.
We are learning that an occupied mind
relinquishes fear from the heart.

And, Lord,

We are thinking about death!

Lord — I'm faced with death's hauntingness, but

I am learning that

it is not fear of death itself,
it is not leaving my family,
it is not relinquishing my body,

it is the UNKNOWN which I fear!

A rustle in the night,
an unseen hand,
a noisy silence,
a cry in the distance.

Lord — who am I to judge what is to come?

Reassure me of thy closeness.
Lift this fear from me!

My child,

let not your heart
be troubled;
ye believe in God,
believe also in me.
I will not leave you
comfortless.
I will come to you.

Thank you, Lord.

I believe.

Without you on my side,
this would be
an endless year, but
because I have YOU,
this will be
just another year
with disappointments
and
discouragements;
and sadness,
and beauty,
and memories.

... and the people beg:
   WHAT'S THE ANSWER, LORD?

It's hard enough to live in a world like this without try-ing to change it. Think how much better life would be if the world were different. What can we do about the mess? We can put it back into the hands of God where it belongs. Then we can become obedient servants, doing what he commands us to do. Until we are ready to let him take over our lives, and our world, we shall only continue to wish things were different. Why not let him show us what he can do with us?

Lord —

> I've been talking with you for a long time.
> I've been trying to listen, too.
> I've thought about the action, Lord,
> But that's not quite so easy!

It means involvement!
It means insecurity!
It means turmoil
in my well-ordered life!

Lord —

I guess I've had myself
at the center of all of this.
And it has to be YOU, Lord.

I've been thinking of MY world, Lord —
But it's really your world, Lord.

I've sensed that YOU understand ME, Lord,
But do I understand YOU?

Things are a mess in this world, Lord.

But they were a mess when
You were here, too, Lord.

Together
can
we really
do something
about it?